MARC CHAGALL

MARC CHAGALL

TEXT BY

MARCEL BRION

OLDBOURNE PRESS
LONDON

PUBLISHED IN BRITAIN 1960
TRANSLATED FROM THE FRENCH
BY A. H. N. MOLESWORTH
© OLDBOURNE BOOK CO. LTD. 1960

PRODUCED BY EDITIONS AIMERY SOMOGY,
PARIS, FRANCE, FOR:
OLDBOURNE PRESS
121 FLEET STREET
LONDON E C 4

THE INVISIBLE REVEALED

In the history of modern painting, Chagall's importance rests mainly on the fact that his work, deliberately removed from the Impressionist tradition, has achieved a completely new approach to modern art without becoming encumbered (except occasionally) by the theoretical problems of so many of today's painters. For Chagall all discussions about "the subject" are meaningless. The importance of the subject in his work depends not on the artist's perception of the experience of reality; it depends on the understanding to be established between the picture as pure painting and the picture as a product of a lively and capricious imagination.

For fifty years, Chagall's painting has achieved a constant and happy state of grace between nature and artist. The subject's autonomy has never constricted the free play of his imagination; neither at any period in the life of the painter, nor anywhere in his works can one find a disagreement or discord between his faithfulness to life and experience and his feeling for the fairylike and the fabulous. In spite of all the "story" depicted, no painting is less "literary". Inspection reveals that the elements of Chagall's painting are not narrative, so that it is not possible to make them form, collectively, a coherent story. Their very incoherency is the best proof of their integrity. If Chagall's magical efflorescence were forced, a rational and causal bond would necessarily be introduced into his work. This is completely absent; total freedom reigns. Anything may enter his compositions: dream figures or products of memory, provided only that their form and tone blend with that of neighbouring objects. Each has its own peculiarities of origin or substance, but each respects the other. Every object is prepared for any changes, internal or external, in substance or in form; a harmonious relationship can then be established with other forms that have been summoned into the picture by the twofold demands of plastic (above all pictorial) and poetic need.

Although he sometimes seems to let his work be governed by unusual creatures of fancy, the painter as creator keeps the upper hand since the picture "is above all a surface, etc. ..." Chagall's singularity, and the unique place of his work in contemporary painting is in his complete indifference to literary content. He makes equally little attempt to achieve, avoid, or submit to the influence of literary content. Detail in his pictures never presents any problem—in the sense that everything is resolved, to begin with, by his extraordinary preliminary orchestration which deals simultaneously with improvisations and complete movements. A Chagall picture always appears to be improvised, and so it is, because up to the last brush-stroke, a bird carrying an umbrella, or a fish climbing a ladder may slip itself in, clothed in the necessary splash of colour, and proving itself indispensable though absurd. For the absurd is nothing more than the logic of dreams and the reasoning of poetry which are in no way related to formal logic or sterile reasoning.

A Chagall painting is a wonderful tree in bloom, perhaps the wak-wak tree of oriental legend, whose flowers take the form of fantastic, incongruous living animals. A Chagall does not conform to normal standards any more than the wak-wak tree conforms to the precepts of botany: both conform only to the laws of miracles. They adhere to that right which all forms and beings have, of taking on the aspect which pleases themselves; for Chagall they have only to suit the picture. In the last analysis it is the picture alone which decides its own existence and its own personality.

Because a Chagall painting is created as a complete and perfect universe, it demands an allegiance which is inevitably moulded to the picture's characteristics. Above all, it demands acceptance of the complete inevitability of its being: inevitability being here the opposite of fortuity. Only the artist, and perhaps not even he, knows why a certain figure appears at a particular moment amongst a group of beings whose mutual bonds are hidden to the spectator. A viewer can only judge the appropriateness of the figure in terms of painting, that is in terms of the balanced and harmonious relation of forms and colours. But it should not be forgotten that a Chagall figure, even if it seems only to have a modest supporting role to play, brings with it a whole range of emotions, feelings, and suggestions, in tune both with the known and the unknown. Each figure plays two parts, the role of a pictorial form and that of a poetic being: since one can never completely unravel its nature and function, the strange privilege of moving at will

7

to and from the realms of mystery gives each figure the weight and majesty assumed by the smallest utterance of a secret language.

Chagall's pictorial vocabulary is a code to which he alone has the key, if he has not forgotten it. The message cannot be systematically deciphered but must be experienced both as an explicit communication and through all its implications. In this respect, it is worthwhile reading the artist's autobiography: he does not reveal all—yet he hints at much. He does not write in this way from any desire to remain cryptic, but because he knows that if his painting is understood, then his message will be revealed. Apart from his painting, everything else about Chagall is enigmatic, but the spectator is not concerned with the enigma, for its solution is the artist's personal problem. This enigma is foreign to the spectator, and it is vain to explain it in terms which would only be valid for a pedestrian outlook. The suddenness with which a Chagall picture grips, conquers and overpowers one, has nothing to do with mere deciphering. The mystery which forms an intimate part of the painting's make-up must not be disturbed. Chagall's work has its own spirit which is itself the explanation and clarification of its mystery.

A Chagall painting need not be approached in a different way from any other painting, but the " œil du cœur " must be wide open, since its function may possibly be more important when looking at a Chagall than with other artists' work. The mind must be open, alert, and prepared to concentrate. The impact of a Chagall is not impaired by a rapid and superficial inspection, because its radiance is perceived clearly and immediately. But to understand the power of all this gaiety, one must live with it and have seen it change, insensibly and

SELF-PORTRAIT. 1909
VALERIE ALPORT COLLECTION, OXFORD

significantly with the hour and the day. Many people disguise themselves as something other than which they are. Chagall disguises himself as himself : in this way he deceives those who search and enquire into him. He repudiates excessive esotericism and refuses to retire as a hermit, and this is the best way of letting it be known that there are many approaches to his art. Between the picture and us there are strange and complicated interlaced designs, stretched in different planes and traced on transparent screens.

Commentators say that there are different ways of reading the same page of the Bible according to the interpretative screen that one lays on it. Perhaps it is the same with Chagall's work. But, we are not here concerned with interpretation. What matters is not what the painting means, but what it is, in all the majesty, grace, beauty and power of its being.

EARLY DAYS IN VITEBSK

Although one must be careful not to take Taine's theory of environment too literally, it is difficult to reach the essence of Chagall's art and his particular idiosyncrasies, if one does not take into account both the circumstances in which his art was formed and the different moral environment with which it has been surrounded. This investigation is not designed to expose the traces of "influences", the discovery of which would diminish the value and quality of his prodigious, undeniable orginality—an originality that stamps so firmly the least of his paintings that the unique spirit of all his work is immediately and unequivocally recognized. It is designed, rather to show Chagall's evolution, during which his indivi-

THE WEDDING IN THE VILLAGE. 1909
BÜHRLE COLLECTION, ZURICH

duality was clearly, vigorously, and surely developed and
defined, despite all the movements into which his curiosity led
him over half a century.

The elements of his pictures, and indeed, his technique, have
been continually and considerably extended and enriched
during the fifty years; they sink their roots deeply and firmly
into the native soil in which they are nourished. While it is not
absolutely necessary to know the biography of an artist in
order to appreciate the quality of his work, in the particular

11

case of Marc Chagall, the art historian inevitably returns, with ever increasing curiosity, to Chagall's family circle and his childhood and adolescent years. The historian does this neither from idle curiosity nor from professional scruples, but because the beings which people his pictures, wrapped in their mystery and exhibited in their nakedness, lie in his childhood treasure house, in the toy cupboard where the adult still ferrets. One can love and admire Chagall without knowing anything of this strange humus of Russian and Jewish folklore which feeds the flower of his fancy. But it is a residual impression to which he always returns to root around for the familiar beings who are magical unfailing sources of amazement, both for him and for the spectator. This is the source from which flows uninterrupted his deliciously extravagant, comic, moving, and sometimes tragic fairyland, always charged with a power of mystery which has lost nothing by being repeated over fifty years. This legendary treasure house, where synagogue chants mingle with Easter Masses, nursemaid's tales, popular ballads, village legends of enchanted animals, miraculous rabbi, and supernatural phenomena, has been built up, brick by brick, in the imagination of those Jewish Communities of Eastern Europe, which were Asiatic enclaves in the lands of the Czar's empire.

When Chagall was born at Vitebsk in July 1887, these communities lived according to their ancient customs. They were faithful to immemorial traditions, and repeated the millennial rituals ; they passed on from generation to generation marvellous and comic stories, the annals of a stupendous past, and the tall stories pedalled from village to village by the ragged wild-eyed tramps with long beards that one meets so often in Chagall pictures. In these closed communities, caught up with the supernatural, but nourished on secular hopes, the ever present feeling for miracle was very intense. No one can help suspecting that every one of these enigmatic, erudite, eloquent vagabonds may be one of those miraculous travelling rabbi whose prodigious feats are innumerable. Perhaps indeed, they represent the prophet Elijah, for whom every Sabbath evening a glass of wine is set at the family table.

Familiarity with the supernatural and the holy is so great that a miracle is no longer even astonishing, so much is it part of daily life. No existence, however modest, can be monotonous for those who know how to look at common objects, how to seek out their hidden souls and how to sense their aura and vitality. Drawing at this twin well of Russian and Jewish tradition so rich in miracles, fables and folk tales, Chagall's memory was filled with all the humble marvels which have retained for him their power of astonishment, rapture, and amusement. Contact with the miraculous presupposes that it moves you by its strangeness, and its unusual and incongruous antics offer innumerable occasions for surprise and amusement. Thus Chagall's fantastic creations, springing from the supernatural, at first terrible and moving, and charged with primitive religious fears, become familiar—like an ogre who becomes friendly as soon as one stops being afraid of him.

The little provincial communities of old Russia were centred upon themselves, cultivating their idiosyncrasies, creating special standards outside common space and time; it was therefore particularly easy for a child to build up myths and legends. In all that he saw, in everything that he heard, Chagall discovered the creatures of his fantastic repertoire, which crowd both his memory and his pictures. He stored up this mass of popular poetry and holy legend, certain that he

I AND THE VILLAGE. 1911
MUSEUM OF MODERN ART, NEW YORK

THE DRINKER. 1911
HANS NEUMANN COLLECTION, CARACAS

would find his toys as alive, as active and as wonderful at whatever age he returned to them.

The word "toy" must not be interpreted arbitrarily; if part of Chagall is playing a game, the game is never merely capricious, nor is it ever free from his essential nature. The toys retain the character that they have for children. Chagall's playthings are important: they have the power of giving birth to prodigies, they are magically fecund, they possess a secret overflowing vitality. His mind and heart are completely devoted to these toys; they are intimately bound up with his very being; they have their outward, secret personalities. They exist in the here-and-now, and at the same time, on other planes, in the invisible perhaps, in another dimension, from which they are able to cast their spells and enchantments. Are they sanctified or bewitched? One doesn't know—perhaps both.

Everything needed to make a poet is here, but it is also material to stimulate a painter. The scenery, violently splashed with gaudy colours, displays the Russian taste for polychromy and for startling colours. In Russian, the same word means both red and beautiful, as though red was considered the quintessence of beauty. Despite the rigorous iconoclastic dogmas, the inherited tradition of oriental splendour ensures that the Torah chest and the brocaded velvets, set off by the gold overlaying the sacred scrolls, sparkle and burn with light and colour in the flickering of wax candles. Perhaps the painter has realized that there are two groups of colours: the profane and the sacred. Profane colours are displayed in shop signs, in the clothes of the Russian peasants coming to market, or in ordinary folk objects on painted wood. The customary monochrome of the countryside, with the dirty white of the snow, the brown log cabins, the grey-brown ploughed fields, the green of spring, emphasizes the least touch of bright colour. It is this touch which gives an air of gala, of richness and even gaiety, to the greyness of roads and meadows. The sacred colours, the purple velvet, the gold of the candelabras and the beautiful Hebrew script, the green-and-gilt church domes, with their elaborate little chains linking the cupolas, form a world apart, connected by symbols to the world of the esoteric and the mysterious. For the artist the association of profane and sacred colours re-establishes the unity of material and spiritual existence, of daily life and the supernatural. It is from this inextricably blended mixture of sacred and profane that Chagall creates his pictures. Thus his feeling for form and colour, and the connexion of his imagination with the object, are no more disassociated and separate, but reunited and wedded in a great burst of fervour and love.

Chagall grew up in an intensely religious atmosphere. If his father exercised the modest functions of assistant in a herring shop, his grandfather was a sacrificial butcher. Religious holidays were celebrated in the family in the spirit of wondering contemplation and ecstatic expectation, so well represented in his *Sabbath* (1909), which records an impression of silent mystical devotion, found every time the memory of Jewish ceremonies returns to his brush.

While quite young Chagall took painting lessons from Pen, a Vitebsk artist, to whom he remained very attached, and who for a long time was his loved and respected counsellor. His parents respected the encouragement given by Pen, and sent the young man to St. Petersburg, where he took a course at the Imperial Academy of Fine Arts.

In St. Petersburg, Repine was the famous master who dominated the art of the period. After a few months of study, Chagall very soon recognized the sterility of a formalist art founded on a narrow conception of realism. Chagall knew that the visible was not the only nor the total reality. He already had his inner urge to enquire into the invisible by means of the visible, not easily expressed through the medium

17

HOMAGE TO APOLLINAIRE. 1911–12
STEDELIJK VAN ABBE-MUSEUM, EINDHOVEN

18

of strict naturalism or academism. If *The Peasant Woman* that he painted in 1907 is a significant example of the aesthetic conformism which menaced the "pre-Chagall Chagall", other contemporary canvases—*The Young Girl on the Sofa* (1907) and *The Small Living Room* (1908)—show a desire for escape already in the process of achievement. This is confirmed by the composition of *The Alley* (1908), which is so bold that it could not have been inspired by any other Russian painter of that period.

The feeling for space, which was so new, shown in *The Small Living Room* and *The Alley,* resulted from two convergent influences which cured Chagall (if he was ever seriously infected) of the virus of social realism. At St. Petersburg, Chagall waxed enthusiastic over the old Russian icon painters' art, which had just been rediscovered about 1905. The frescoes of the churches and *Lavras,* the processional icons of the masters of the schools of Pskov, Moscow, and Novgorod which had been ignored and unrecognized for a long time, had at last attracted the cognoscenti. The masterpieces of Maxim the Greek, Master Denis, Roublev, and Theopanus the Greek were revered by tradition with a veneration as much religious as artistic.

It would be wrong to imagine Chagall as developing in isolation, unconnected with the great streams of Western art. Current French painting was well understood and correctly appraised by the Russians of 1909. Young artists like Chagall and Soutine were in the forefront of those who sought to understand and study the bold revolution in France. This does not mean that either was tempted to imitate. In a spirit and technique which owe nothing to French inspiration, Chagall continued to paint scenes of Jewish Life in Provincial Towns:

THE WEDDING. 1910

20

THE ARTIST'S COLLECTION

21

The Musicians (1907), *The Dead Man* (1908), *The Village Fair* (1908); these keep all their local savour, their spontaneity, and their simultaneous drama and irony. Nevertheless, the contact with the Parisian masters decided Chagall to continue his researches in the city where modern painting was developing. Fortunately, Deputy Vinaver, who had already provided the necessary means for his study at St. Petersburg, procured further funds sufficient for him to continue his apprenticeship in Paris. Vinaver realized how indispensable this sojourn was to enable the young painter to blossom.

PARIS 1910—13

Installed at the Ruche, that picturesque artists' colony in the middle of Paris, in the dilapidated rooms of a former exhibition hall, Chagall found himself plunged into a boiling crucible where new forms and bold ideas were being developed. It was an exhilarating epoch. In the turbulent activity of European painting around 1910, the Fauve movement reached an almost classical stature, Cubism dissected and reconstructed the surface planes and appearance of objects, Futurism inaugurated a new representation of movement, while Orphism christened by Guillaume Apollinaire broke down light rays into their own chromatic content—a content at once scientific and inspired.

It was the period when Apollinaire wrote *Les Peintres Cubistes* and when Marinetti exploded his futurist manifestos; the first appeared in the *Figaro* of 20 February 1909, followed two months later by *Tuons le clair de lune*. The whole traditional conception of form was severely shaken. Modern painting, with a kind of drunken clarity, blazed an unknown trail through a forest of strict doctrinaire systems, and irresistible creative urges. "It was the purity, the chemistry of painting which drew me to France. Before I reached Paris my bread had neither salt nor pepper." In his autobiography

THE CATTLE DEALER. 1912
KUNSTMUSEUM, BASEL

Chagall recalls the strong emotional impact that this ferment of activity made on him and on his art. Quite naturally he formed connections with the artists that he felt were closest to him, the Cubists—La Fresnaye, Delaunay, Gleizes, and Léger. In turn Soutine, who had left Minsk, arrived in Paris in 1911.

Cubism emerged as the boldest and most revolutionary movement. At one blow it swept away Academism and Impressionism, and concentrated on the problems of formal structure. Although Chagall could not completely adopt the ideas laid down by Apollinaire and Gleizes and although he was by character and temperament closer to the Futurists than the Cubists, the discipline imposed by the Cubist school attracted him. Their example encouraged him to enquire again into the treatment of form as such. He never pursued the implications of form as an absolute to their logical conclusion, but the lessons were of value to him, if only as an experiment.

The famous *Homage to Apollinaire* (1911–12), the *Self-Portrait with Seven Fingers* (1911), *Adam and Eve* (1912), *The Poet or Half Past Three* (1911) or *From the Moon* (1911) are, in effect, experiments in the dissection and reconstruction of forms composed according to the demands of Cubist doctrines. In these paintings Chagall never wandered far from his centre of inspiration—from his lyric fantasy—but he treated the products of the fantasy in a paradoxical style, freer than that of "scientific" Cubism. In reality he was very far from Picasso's austere dialectic, or from Braque's classic Constructivism and far even from Delaunay's Simultaneism: he was almost as far from them as were the social or romantic Realists Levitan, Vroubel and Mossatow whom he had formerly admired. The essential strength of his personality is that it never allows him to drift aside from the road which he has consciously or unconsciously chosen. Chagall is an example of an artist who has passed through all the great European artistic movements between 1910 and 1923, from Fauvism to the Bauhaus. He has known them, at first hand, studied and experimented with them, and contemplated them from a distance, but he has never, even for the shortest moment, been untrue to his own unshakeable originality.

His integrity is not a negative quality. It is not the result of ignorance or refusal. No painter of this age has made such a sensitive response to, or remained so constantly alive and alert to, all the appeals of the European "schools". Yet he has only absorbed those of their teachings which were best adjusted to his personality and those which would fuse with his art. He is completely the opposite of a systematist or a doctrinaire. Although he well understands the *système* in art, he has great plasticity and he never withdraws into an ivory tower out of reach of other painters' influence. However, the lessons of Cubism penetrated him to a certain extent, sharpened his curiosity, and stimulated his taste for novelty : Cubism also probably helped him to know himself better and to further the stocktaking of his personal resources. The *Still Life* (1912) is completely Cézanne in spirit, but treated with a feeling for space absolutely different from that of the Master of Aix. All the same, the effort that has been made to trace the bizarre composition *Adam and Eve* to the influences of Marcel Duchamp and Boccioni—a curious association in this respect —only serves to illuminate more clearly its special, uniquely Chagall, quality.

It should be pointed out that it was not strictly speaking a plastic requirement that forced him to add two complementary fingers to the *Self-Portrait* (1911), called *The Painter with Seven Fingers,* but a simple flight of fancy, exactly of the same order as that which decapitated the farmer's wife whom he is in course of painting, and projected her head into space. It was the same spirit, in fact, which animated the picture of the same year, *To Russia, Asses and Others* (1911),

THE YELLOW RABBI. 1912
PRIVATE COLLECTION, KREFELD

ADAM AND EVE. 1912
CITY ART MUSEUM OF ST. LOUIS   27

in which the treatment of forms followed the Cubist dissection, not simply in obedience to a dogma of construction but through a spirit of fun impelled by the incongruous welling up within him. Perhaps his composition had some functional value also, for it disposed the different masses more harmoniously through the different areas of the painting.

Although he found himself in an environment quite different from that to which he was used, and though attracted by all the aesthetic experiments which were going on around him, Chagall was never uprooted. He had signed his provisional declaration of allegiance to Cubism, in painting the *Homage to Apollinaire* in which he added the names of Riciotto Lanudo, Blaise Cendrars and Herwarth Walden, to the name of the poet of *Alcools*. Walden edited the review *Der Sturm* in Berlin which, together with his exhibitions, exercised a notable influence on the development of German art. Already Paris had become, as it has always remained, the meeting point of all national and international artistic movements, the centre on which artists of every continent converged, the laboratory where they communicated and exchanged their discoveries. One also notes in the composition of this painting something which is not a " manifesto ", but rather a Cubist mandorla, reminiscent of Robert Delaunay's *Cercles*.

The abundant, magnificent output of Chagall's first Parisian period was only partly dedicated to formal problems (if one can say these problems are ever absent from any work of art), that is, dedicated to a formalism analogous to that proclaimed and practised by Cubism, Futurism and Simultaneism. With Chagall the problem never found a solution, firstly because pictorial demands directed his attention to the plastic, and secondly because the controlling imagination of dreams plays a greater part in his composition than does constructive logic. The problems which were presented in this first Paris period were in fact, for the most part, the extension of the questions of free will, instinct, and the unconscious, which were posed at St. Petersburg, and at Vitebsk itself. The best proof of this is that the old faithful themes imposed themselves on him and returned. They are inseparable from the artist because in all probability they were not chosen by him but imposed upon him. Presented with other plastic and pictorial means, they offered themselves to his fantasy for orchestration into new melodies. It was the orchestration that changed, richer, freer and easier in the disposition of the means recently acquired : the spirit which governed invention and composition remained the same. *The Holy Drosky Driver* (1911) springing from Hassidic tradition, *The Pregnant Woman* (1913), *The Violinist* (1911–14), *The Yellow Rabbi* (1912) emerge directly from the Jewish folklore of Eastern Europe. In the same year that he painted the *Homage to Apollinaire* as a token of gratitude, and in part at least of acquiescence to Parisian Cubism, he painted another canvas, *I and the Village* (1911), which is so characteristically Chagall. It was composed in the manner of an orthodox Cubist painting but at the same time reached beyond with his almost unbridled freedom of arrangement and handling, in Russian style.

The pull of Vitebsk, of its farms, its *isbahs,* its donkeys and cows, was nothing nostalgic, it was simply the manifestation of the close bond between the artist and this familiar world which he carries with him everywhere, to Paris, to Berlin, to Moscow, and to the United States. It travels with him because it is his inner world, the world of images born of desire perhaps rather than of memory ; a world of violent and emotional

THE MUSICIAN. 1912–13
STEDELIJK MUSEUM, AMSTERDAM

subjectivity, of the same nature as that where dream people dwell, but charged to the limit with that realism of which the inventions of our imagination become capable when they possess absolute integrity. This free original lyricism blossoming in a wondrous riot of colour remained the basis of all the work of this period. But at this time he also executed the very strange spatial compositions of *The Birth* (1911) and *The Yellow Room* (1911), where the third dimension, escaping from traditional perspective, is located in an incorporeal, unreal, almost metaphysical space, which is developed into another plane—perhaps that of a vision or dream.

The formal edifice constructed by the Cubists remained within the realms of logic and possibility. For Chagall, there was no order but subversion ; there was a reversal of the natural laws, an arbitrary and almost abstract projection of the elements of the picture which is purely irrational, though his plastic feeling was always harmoniously attuned to imagination's whims. The illogicality which controls our dreams has its own laws—laws not those of waking life. *From the Moon* (1911) is the most striking example of this incongruous reorganization. It displays a rare harmony of forms and colours ; the appurtenances of Vitebsk folklore, the moon, the *isbah,* the goat, the farmer, the *traktir*, replace the guitar and the rum bottle of Braque, Picasso, or Juan Gris. Yet it possesses another life, mysterious, supernatural, autonomous, which favours all plastic deformation, and which exhibits all the caprices of the childish fantasy that arranges the pieces of his construction game with a loving knowledge of the balance of masses and the lyricism of colour.

Chagall's first stay in Berlin lasted only a few months. The artist cut it short to return to Vitebsk, where he married Bella, whose admirable portraits, overwhelming the spectator by the passion which animates them, are a survey of her life. Bella alive, and, still more, Bella dead, lives in his work, peoples his pictures, becoming the soul of the landscape, the Shulamite of the Song of Songs. Aesthetically, this first visit to Berlin put

OVER VITEBSK. 1914
SAM ZACK COLLECTION, TORONTO

Chagall in contact with artists whom he had not had the opportunity to know in Russia, and met very little in Paris: the Expressionists—Klee, whose imagination was as free as his own, Campendonck, resembling him in thought and art, and the admirable draughtsman Alfred Kubin, a formidable explorer in visionary gloom.

In Paris, Chagall had exhibited at the Salon des Indépendants, among the Cubists. Herwarth Walden opened the doors of *Der Sturm* Gallery to him, where he found himself hung beside Klee for his first exhibition, beside Kubin for the second, and finally alone in the showing of June 1914. From this last dates Chagall's huge and enduring success in Germany. As a reaction against the naturalism of Uhde, the Impressionism of Liebermann, the post-romantic realism of Leible and Trubner, the Expressionists threw themselves into the breach formed by Louis Corinth, Edvard Munch, and Van Gogh. Imagination was given complete freedom; free handling of colour was carried to a paroxysm of frenzy which destroyed form; dramatic feeling controlled formal considerations, and the explosive and the unconscious replaced the arranged and the contrived. Expressionist anarchy was not a system as was Cubism, it obeyed only the irresistible force of untrammelled instinct.

The enthusiastic reception that Expressionist Germany gave the first Chagall exhibitions proved that she found in him a painter after her own heart, a member of her true artistic family. As far as Chagall himself was concerned, he had achieved the thing that the Expressionists were striving for, the tension of pathos that he had already displayed for seven years. It was not contrived, but given, received as a present from heaven, a state of grace communicating with the invisible, with the talent of bringing to light the host of waiting dreams

that besieged him. Thus the atmosphere of Berlin was less stimulating than that of Paris, despite the presence of the great German artists, or of their work: Franz Marc, August Macke, Kokoschka, and Kandinsky (who exhibited two years previously at the same gallery), and the members of *Die Brücke*, Nolde, Heckel, Kirchner, Schmidt-Rottluff, and Pechstein.

The turbulence and ferment were no less intense and the activity no less fecund in the crucible of Berlin than in that of Paris; one can rediscover it in the very fine *Self-Portrait* (1914), and in *The Mother in front of the Stove* (1914) as well as in the *Smolensk Gazette* (1914). Whether these pictures dated the same year were painted in Germany or Russia does not much matter: they are remarkable for the lack of Chagall's usual magical feeling and must be considered as a prelude to the period of objectivity when his fantasy grew more sober, and which gave birth to *Strawberries* (1916) and the *Portrait of Ida and Bella in front of the Window* (1916).

RETURN TO RUSSIA 1915—22

The war held Chagall in Russia where he had arrived to get married in July 1914. It cut him off from the rest of the world for some years, but this re-establishment in Russia was a most valuable experience, for the artist found himself in the presence of political events which overawed and went beyond private destiny. It led him, too, to join in a collective action which up to that moment had seemed to be completely foreign to his spirit. The October Revolution searched for scenery painters among the avant-garde for its celebrations and monuments. Chagall was noted and chosen as Commissar of Fine Arts

35

THE YOUNG GIRL ON HORSEBACK. 1929
GEORGES DAELMANS COLLECTION, BRUSSELS

for the district of Vitebsk. In this post he was responsible for
the reorganization of art instruction. From his experience at
the St. Petersburg Academy, he had discovered how inadequate,
backward, and little informed the academic world was about
the current movements in France, Germany, and Italy. Chagall
was also concerned with the museums, which he renovated.

◁ THE LOVERS IN GREEN. 1916–17
PRIVATE COLLECTION

inspired, and to which he gave a more active life. Finally, he undertook to collect together all the modern artists in Russia to get them to collaborate in the development of an aesthetic worthy of the new age.

Russia has rarely, if ever, since the great era of the icon painters of Pskov, Novgorod, and Moscow, possessed so much original and powerful talent. In these revolutionary years Russian art was revealed as one of the boldest pioneers of form and thought. It was in fact in Russia that Kandinsky achieved the great step from representation to abstraction, and where Malevitch founded, with Suprematism, his theme of white emptiness, which corresponded to a sort of mystical denudation, a material vacuum ready to receive the effusions and products of the spirit. At the same moment, Constructivism rejected all sentimentality, all narrative, and, simultaneously, all reference to the real. The Constructivists founded their art on an ascetic geometry, stripping form so that it became at once a pure plastic object and a pure product of intelligence. The rigidity of the elimination achieved by Tatlin, Lissitzky, Pevsner, and Gabo gave a firm solid foundation to Abstraction. At the same time, the *Rayonisme* of Larionov and Gontcharova, encouraged and blessed by Apollinaire in 1914, introduced to Russia an acclimatized version of Paris Cubism and Milan Futurism.

At this period few countries were as fitted as Russia to become the cradle both of an unprecedented transformation of modern aesthetics and of the techniques of painting and sculpture. This brief flowering, rich in so much promise, did not, at least in Russia, last long : the great innovators did not hesitate to emigrate ; most of them transplanted their art to Berlin or Paris. But they were each already isolated, materially and spiritually. All common discipline had gone by the board

—if one can speak of discipline with reference to Cubism and Futurism. Dissensions quickly sprang up around Chagall, and amongst the artists he had collected. They sprang precisely from the aesthetic isolation of each, from the strength of the ideological position which each had taken up, from the impossibility of collecting over a common denominator such fiercely irreconcilable individualities as Malevitch and Lissitzky ; perhaps political considerations, which are not considered here, were also mixed up in it. However, after the short Futurist euphoria of the Soviet regime, art which did not show enough social responsibility was tainted by the suspicion of freedom.

Initiative soon failed and the disillusioned artists emigrated and dispersed. This little book is not about the history of Russia in the years which followed after 1917 ; it is only concerned with the personal destiny of Chagall. The way in which his mind and his technique reacted to his return to his native town is characteristic of the strong, authentic individuality to which the works of the preceding years are witness, whether they were painted at Vitebsk, St. Petersburg, Paris, or Berlin. If Chagall's art is in constant turmoil, stirred by incessant transformations in the treatment of form and colour, it rests none the less on a foundation of unchangeable ideas of which the chief element is what might be called his visionary realism. This is something quite different from the Surrealist aesthetic which from time to time has claimed him as its own, although he has no connexion with it, and has knowingly turned his back on it. Chagall has no need to call on the unusual to dispel the banality of everyday life, because banality does not exist for him. Everything which is ordinary is simultaneously extraordinary, or capable of becoming so. This world in the centre of which he lives has always been, and continues to be, an

THE LOVERS ON THE ROOF. 1927–28
MUSÉES ROYAUX DES BEAUX-ARTS, BRUSSELS

THE ACROBAT. 1930
MUSÉE NATIONAL D'ART MODERNE, PARIS   41

enchanted world. The mechanism of the association of ideas functions, in his fantasy, in exactly the same way as it does in Russian folk tales; an *isbah* is an indisputable material object, a chicken's feet are also unquestionably material objects: that the *isbah* should climb onto the chicken's feet and start to run becomes an event, mysterious, supernatural, but whose components are firmly material. Thus Chagall's fantasy, as will be seen later, always holds closely and intimately to the reality intrinsic to the object, but remains equally real in its invisible aura, the infra-red and ultra-violet areas that surround the object.

While the Russian period of 1917–22 saw Chagall's aesthetic develop all the multiple manifestations of which it was capable, he did not at any time exhibit a tendency to come to terms, aesthetically that is, with Suprematism or Constructivism. Although Chagall's art has always been susceptible to influence, permeable by and receptive to the great currents of contemporary painting, it remained as isolated in Russia as it was in France and Germany. None of the lessons which he learnt in Paris and Berlin were forgotten, but all were harmoniously blended with his radical Chagallism, which clings to his spirit and his art as his skin clings to his flesh. In the deepening of his visionary imagination, in the enrichment and clarification of his technique, his art continued its internal and external evolution along the furrow that he had already ploughed. This Russian stay, like the other periods of his life, is exempt from all systematization, which is why all his works present the combination of unity and variety that always distinguishes them. It is this combination that reveals the inextinguishable fecundity of his experiments. If one puts on one side the curious *Goat Composition* (1917) which has echoes recalling

THE CIRCUS HORSEWOMAN. 1931
FORMERLY REGNAULT COLLECTION, LAREN

Klee, and studies three typical paintings, one notices how he has extended and amplified his Cubist experiments. *No Matter Where Outside the World* (1919) again takes up the theme of the head cut in two, the top half separated from its axis and turned towards an inverted townscape. No doubt the severed head has some secret meaning. But it is interesting to observe the technique by which the body is dissected formally into geometrical planes cut and contrasted in such a way as to obtain a very strong expression of pure plasticity. In contrast, the *Cubist Landscape* (1918), unique exception in the whole of Chagall's work, appears as a sort of divertimento, a scherzo, a consciously designed pastiche of the Cubists' *papiers collés*. The canvas gives the illusion of a *collage* with its false woods, its false linoleum, its false *papier froissé*. It is an admirably successful touch, a supremely refined *trompe l'œil*, with its marvellous colouring, and its delicate tones, its exquisite glistening quality. In the middle of this abstract structure the Chagallian fantasy reappears with the intrusion of a little man under an umbrella, who, at the formal focus of the composition, is the only living being in a geometrical universe. The third Cubist picture is *The Cemetery Gate* (1917) with its splendid, strange, and overpowering harmony in supernatural green. The pillars and the pedimented lintel covered with Hebrew script shining mysteriously like the words of a magic spell are brought out in relief from a truly fantastic atmosphere by the breakdown of space into luminous planes like the rays from an aberrant projector. Here one finds oneself thrown into the extraordinary world of Hassidic legends where, outside the daily round, miracles abound. It is the world of Golem and Dybbouk, part of the repertoire of the Moscow Jewish Theatre where Chagall was invited to paint walls, curtains, and scenery.

For this painting the artist did not have to make any effort to rediscover the atmosphere of supernatural mysticism which was already the substance of his art. The tragedy and the humour of the dramas and comedies forming the basis of this theatre already belonged to his heart and soul; but his own inner theatre dominated him exclusively, and would not allow him to express himself as an actual theatre decorator. And while later (in 1942 and 1945) he painted the scenery for *Aleko* and *The Firebird* for the Americans, it was his own fairyland, his personal magic, that flourished there.

Formal problems, however, dominated and controlled the fantasies of his imagination; nothing is less automatic than the fantasy which is contained by a composition vigorously harmonized to the given space. In *The Reclining Poet* (1915) the landscape is built on a sort of predella formed by the prostrate man at the foot of the picture; but the most remarkable phenomenon is the animation displayed by a figure constrained in a space as confined as the face of a Romanesque capital. The first study in oil and crayon for *Man Leaping over City (En Avant)* (1917) and the gouache *The Painter* (1916) represent to perfection the painter's aptitude for representing, when the opportunity arises, a lively, rapid movement, in the form of an arabesque—which under the brush of another would be merely decorative.

The portrait *Bella with a White Collar* (1917) must stand out as a perfect example of his visionary realism which idealizes the individual portrayed to superhuman dimensions, endowing the sitter with an almost divine presence. It is perhaps the most beautiful and most moving of the great variety of portraits of his wife, each of which displays such balanced and magnificent grandeur. It is in fact possible to

THE WHITE CRUCIFIXION. 1938
THE ART INSTITUTE OF CHICAGO

pursue an instructive study of Chagall's style by considering only the different portraits of Bella, from *The Fiancée with Black Gloves* (1909), the *Bella with Carnation* (1925) to the *Bella in Green* (1934), without counting the innumerable compositions in which Bella appears, more or less recognizable. It is the same tender visionary poetry that is evident in the *Portrait of Vava* (1953–56).

Everything in the form of sensation or emotion that has entered Chagall's world at one time, remains there on the different planes of the conscious and the unconscious. There it is transformed, sends down its roots much as a seed germinates in the soil, and brings forth extraordinary flowers. Technically and pictorially it is very difficult to establish different periods in Chagall's work, unless we mark them by the ever greater lightening of his palette, and the increasing levity of his matter, leading to the extreme fluidity of Paris in 1953–55 and recent *gouaches*. As for the rest, the initial essential content of the parcel containing the emotions and images which he carries with him has remained unchanged.

It would be arbitrary to fix on 1923, the year of his final return to Paris, as marking the end of the years of apprenticeship, because this master has kept an appetite for learning and an apprentice's curiosity. A man's apprenticeship is never ended, still less that of an artist. Therefore, it would be absurd to say that Chagall's style was fixed once the early years were over, because he never stopped evolving and changing. Considering particularly the problem of his impasto and colour, one notices that the warm and sensual richness of the material is always closely allied to the startling freedom of the yellows, reds, and blues in this chromatic orchestration which vibrates with such extraordinary emotional power. In passing, one

THE WALL OF LAMENTATION. 1932
MUSEUM, TEL AVIV

should notice how he finds subtle, celestial shades from his
palette when he is in fact portraying an *Angel at the Palette*
(1927–36), whose wings and garments shine with sparkling
iridescence, a passage of a refinement rare even in the work
of this painter so well versed in every refinement of " painting ".
Although it would be wrong to speak of Chagall's work other

48

than in terms of painting, the study of his art invites the elucidation of the final anecdotal or esoteric meaning of the figures which return almost with the frequency of an obsession. But Heaven prevent us trying to psychoanalyze Chagall!

It might be supposed that he himself invites us to consider his painting from this angle as well, since he has said, "Everything in art should correspond to the flow of our blood, to our whole being, even the unconscious." Perhaps we should attempt to revalue, or at least rehabilitate "Mysticism"—from which so many painters recoil in horror.

SOLITUDE. 1933
MUSEUM, TEL AVIV

ENCHANTED REALISM

"People are wrong to be afraid of this word 'Mysticism', they give it too orthodox a religious interpretation. The antiquated mildewy exterior must be stripped from this term; it must be interpreted in its original, pure, elevated, intact sense. Mysticist ... how many times have people thrown that word in my face as before they used to reproach me with being literary. But would there be a single great picture, a single great poem or even a great social movement in the world without mysticism?" Thus wrote Chagall in 1945 in the review *Renaissance* (Free School of Higher Study, New York). The true, objective source that gives rise to this fairyland so solidly anchored in mind and matter is revealed by reading his autobiography *Ma Vie*. That which appears bizarre and incongruous to the onlooker approaching his pictures with the desire to explain everything in terms of reason, is nothing but the poetic and pictorial transposition of an event which has struck the artist. By the return of impressions and emotions a banal fact is transformed into a sort of fantastic phenomenon: this is precisely because the function of the childish imagination is to project the events of everyday life into the realm of the fabulous and unknown.

Chagall often quotes Rembrandt; he claims a close affinity with him, less in style than in the effect achieved by both artists when they render reality in mythical terms. If one delves into Chagall's sources (the sources of his formal vocabulary rather than his sense of material and colour), into his mode of expressing the fantastic, and into the contents of these fables, one finds them in the transmutations effected by the sensibility of a very lively child. It is a mind wide open to all sensations, enraptured with poetry and music, participating in an over-heated religious atmosphere, where every object that holds his glance or falls to his touch is revealed as susceptible to enchantment.

Most often he is a beneficent magician; Chagall's fantasy is never terrifying, at least never immediately so, only on reflection. In their exaltation his unusual creations are metaphors comparable to Biblical lyricism and to the rabbi's chants sung at family prayers. All his creations are generated from objects with the most prosaic appearance, for an object in which an extraordinary potentiality is not innate does not exist. Chagall really saw the old man sitting on the roof, the old man really was his father. The feeling of enthusiasm that seized his father when he heard music or was particularly joyful is represented by his head leaving his body and flying out into space. The gigantically proportioned violinist is Uncle Neuch who " played like a cobbler " ; *The Manager* (1925), in Charles de Noaille's collection, is mentioned in *Ma Vie,* as Chagall's first memory as a very small child. If Chagall has illustrated La Fontaine perfectly, it is because the animals which roamed the Jewish quarter of Vitebsk were at one and the same time fabulous and commonplace. His cocks, pigs, and cows come directly from the cowshed and the farmyard; thence they have entered into his pictures without losing anything of their objective attributes; they have also acquired a transparency which enables one to penetrate their innocent animal souls, and to glimpse the mystery they contain.

Chagall was right not to wish to be assimilated by the Surrealists; their fantasy is clearly distinct from his own aptitude for childish sorcery and poetic supernaturalism. Nor, since he needed real objects, and because his formal problems, of struc-

51

BETWEEN DOG AND WOLF. 1938–43
IDA MEYER-CHAGALL COLLECTION, BERN

A Summer Night's Dream. 1939
Musée de Peinture et de Sculpture, Grenoble 53

ture and composition, were subordinated to imagination, could he align himself with Cubism. The musicality of his colour and his exuberant palette, rendered so varied and delicately vibrant by the Midi, corresponds above all to a certain internal harmony. From this spring the dream bouquets of *Red Flowers* (1950), *Almond Trees* (1955–56), *White Window* (1955), the profuse bouquet of *Beautiful Redhead*, or the even more extraordinary *Flying Fish* (1948).

Chagall, like Bonnard, was inspired by the Midi. The resultant fireworks dissolved form into an exquisite shimmering of colour, into chromatic harmonies which are really pure painting pushed to the extremes of freedom and joy. Chagall knows he has nothing to fear from literary painting, because he is first of all, before everything else, in his conscious and in his unconscious being, a painter's painter; even his drawings and his engravings in black and white are subtly and vigorously coloured. Further, it is by the transposition of pictorial characteristics into the third dimension that his sculpture affirms its plastic quality—as in *King David, Fish and Woman* (1952), and *Adam and Eve* (1953).

The study of a large composition that is representative of these coloured fireworks reveals how his painting has become increasingly free from all thickness and heaviness. This is exemplified by *The Big Circus* (1956). This painting is a chromatic tone-poem, a symphony, magnificently constructed and developed, that culminates in the apotheosis of fantasy and colour. Here are the fish climbing the ladder, the double being, the hermaphrodite whose two upper halves of the body unite at the waist, the violin bird, the man with a he-goat's head, the amorous Pan bearing a bouquet of flowers, the lion carrying an umbrella posed like the lions of Judah that are carved on

the chests containing the Torah in the synagogue; these, together with the acrobats and the tightrope walkers, are the
mysterious companions who have accompanied the artist from
childhood.

THE REVOLUTION. 1937
THE ARTIST'S COLLECTION

This painting is not just the synthesis of all the other compositions based on the circus, *The Acrobat* (1914), *The Acrobat*
(1930), *The Harlequins* (1922–44), *The Blue Circus* (1950–52),
and the mysterious *Clowns of the Night* (1957). In a sumptuous,

55

playful spirit inspired by the very theme of circus he has collected together his enchanted creatures. It is a world abounding with antics, comical surprises, and exquisite treasure-troves of colour: the spangled tutu of the girl on the horse, the dark purple halo surrounding the piano, the yellow and blue Janus in the bottom left corner of the canvas. The spectator wonders whether these fabulous objects have or have not had a real and factual existence in the artist's life, and it is hard to repress the temptation to investigate the ultimate esoteric meaning of forms and colours as has been done with the great myth creators Bosch and Blake.

MYTHOLOGICAL VOCABULARY

A painter is not always ready to interpret his extraordinary language in terms of ordinary speech. His grammar is provided by the transformation undergone by images and sensations received by the conscious and unconscious memory. The images which are not conserved as such are deposited in the secret cells of the memory, which works alone, unknown to the artist, and transforms, masks and sublimates them. These images and sensations change their nature; they grow or, rather, they are concentrated, condensed and clothed in a fantastic garb which, however, does not conceal their ordinary contours and volumes. The translation from reality to myth, the means by which the real becomes the mythical, gives it a symbolic value, the potentiality of a hieroglyph, a magical number. It is like the pentagon which becomes a pentacle when the correct letters of the spell have been written within it.

This magic power of the incantation makes the spells of

ABRAHAM AND THE THREE ANGELS. 1931–40–50
PRIVATE COLLECTION

sorcerers and miraculous rabbis possible, breathes life into a clay image, creates a " golem " of it, or kills this same " golem " by changing only one letter of the incantation. This power overwhelms the onlooker confronted by the fantastic properties of compositions where objective reality, transformed within itself and saturated with passion, dreams, and poetry generates its greatest force, the power of mystery. One is led to wonder whence these fantastic beings emanate. In *Ma Vie,* Chagall relates that they originate in his childhood at Vitebsk. In this book, although he does not expressly discourage them, he does not invite attributions of esoteric significance. Inasmuch as the image is in itself both a plastic and a pictorial fact, one ought not to be led to deduce that the image only obeys formal necessity, or that it is the result of pure caprice. With an artist like Chagall, a third factor, to be added to the formal and the capricious, is the individual mythology that a very imaginative mind naturally creates for itself. In a closed world, violently agitated internally, such as the Jewish community of Eastern Europe, this individual mythology becomes grafted on to the common stock. Generations of synagogue cantors, of rabbis (others may have been as miraculous as Rabbi Israel Eliezer, who was known as the Baal Chem Tov, or the Magguid de Mezritch, or Rabbi Yaakob Yitzshak de Pzysha, or the Seer of Lublin . . .), generations of humble Jews, poor, modest, hardworking and pious, permeated by the wonderful recitative which sprouted like a jungle around the Bible and the Talmud, over-excited by the supernatural atmosphere of synagogue feasts, and the weekly marvel of the Holy Sabbath at the family table—all these generations culminated and, indeed, were reborn in the creations of Marc Chagall.

Amongst a people who enquire indefatigably into the destiny

58

of men and humanity, and whose penetrating, restless intelligence works without respite on religious problems, the polyvalence of signs and images is a tradition. There is no question of making a straightforward interpretation of the symbols of this mythological vocabulary, because they are not straightforward, rather, they are more than they seem. There is no reason why the waggon that passes in the muddy street, between houses so low that in certain places the carriage seems to roll over the roofs, should not leave the roofs to fly off into space. Perhaps, under its common appearance, this flying cart might be the prophet Elijah's chariot come to carry him off to heaven.

The street lamp that splits its standard into two and walks, the musical instrument that becomes its own musician and plays itself, and the animal musician known to Romanesque sculptors and the painters of ancient Egypt, are images that belong to the common stock of mythology. The being that floats in the air, and walks on the clouds as comfortably as on the earth, is a common dream figure, catalogued and interpreted by necromancers. The cleft head that joins two hostile or simply different faces, the body that develops into a hermaphrodite, the head that flies off like a balloon, all these are found in the common library of nocturnal or waking dreams. A clock is a familiar object, whose tick-tock brings it strangely to life; to a child who listens to it in the dark silence of his room, it is not in itself mysterious; perhaps for Chagall it is nothing more than a memory—"The grandfather clock was always there," he said. But when the clock returns (in the sense that one speaks of the return of a ghost) in so many compositions (although this does not indicate that the clock has acquired the character of an obsession), some of the mystical appurtenances of this symbol of passing time force themselves upon one. Wings may be grafted on the wooden case; the pendulum is always significant, either placed on a diagonal as a sign of perpetual movement or held vertical as a sign that time has stopped—death. There are many of these clock compositions: *The Grandfather Clock* (1914), huge, almost filling the whole canvas, relegating the person sitting in front of a window to a corner; *Time is a River without Banks* (1930–39); *Self-Portrait with a Clock* (1947), where the clock throws itself into space with wide-open arms. One of the most remarkable is *The Clock with a Blue Wing* (1949), whose glass-windowed case contains a couple of lovers beside the stopped pendulum: it is placed like a star in the night sky, above the little snow-covered town, through which the old pedlar strides (might he be the Wandering Jew?). So many of Chagall's canvases require the spectator to look beyond the obvious facts for a symbol or a symbol association that might betray a complete philosophy of life at once serious and dramatic.

Is it legitimate to question Chagall's work on matters which do not arise directly from his painting? Does one not thereby needlessly risk complicating the physiognomy of the artist whom Lionello Venturi has described as "a simple soul"? This leads one to question even the notion of simplicity, where fantasy is concerned. Chagall is simple in that he dwells quite naturally, that is to say singlemindedly, in a world of fantasy. Chagall lives in a world without shadows, and the clarity of his mind is reflected in his limpid painting. It is this quality of clarity that is recalled by the words of Jacques Maritain, who referred to his *saine clarté*.

APPEARANCE OF THE ARTIST'S FAMILY. 1935–47
THE ARTIST'S COLLECTION

62

THE CLOCK WITH A BLUE WING. 1949
IDA MEYER-CHAGALL COLLECTION, PARIS

THE BIBLE EPICS

Vollard wished to add a Bible illustrated by Chagall to his *Ames Mortes* and his *Fables de La Fontaine*. This commission led the artist to consider the Holy Scriptures from a new angle. Although Gogol's masterpiece was particularly sympathetic to the specifically Russian element of his character, it was too prosaic and too anecdotal; and the rational, pedestrian animals in the *Fables* were too much like men since they lacked the fantasy which animated the magic creatures of Vitebsk. In the Bible, however, Chagall should have been able to feel at home. It cannot be denied that Chagall's Russian Judaism was closely linked to the Bible. The spirit of the beautiful, miraculous stories of another age shines through his pictures even when they do not seem directly inspired by a Biblical source. In this, the most complex and most fantastic of books, suffused with the breath of the spirit, all mystical storms rage. It is the supreme lesson of the relation between God and Man since the creation is expounded through divers symbols displayed at overlaying depths. Direct contact with the Holy Land gave new resonance and a wider spiritual horizon to Chagall. In 1931 in Palestine, he discovered the true home of his ancestors, the earthly Jerusalem for which each Jewish community in Western Europe cultivated a nostalgia while creating the ideal New Jerusalem. A new Chagall was born of this meeting with the Holy Land; and in the diligent research that followed his reading of the Bible with a view to its plastic interpretation, he found the world of epic and heroic legend opened before him, a world to which he had not until then had immediate access.

No Bible illustrator has yet been able to reveal the hidden

meaning of the Scriptures by rendering them in pictures, nor was Chagall the enlightened visionary who could achieve this. He contented himself with exploring Biblical history. It should be understood that even in history the natural and supernatural intermingle and blend to the point of becoming indistinguishable. On the level of fanciful reality, angels and men exchange forms and sit down at the same table. The spirit of miracle is felt through the howling of the storm, in the cracking of the burning bush, in the rustling of seraphic wings studded with thousands of eyes, and in the grinding of devilish jaws: but the evocation of the invisible is so well executed in terms of the visible that there is no lack of harmony between the human and the divine, the earth-bound and the marvellous.

The picture of *Abraham and the Three Angels* has three successive versions: the first dates from 1931, the others from 1940 and from 1950. It is perhaps the first painting based strictly on Bible history, and was born of Chagall's new conception of the Bible provoked by Vollard's commission and the visit to Palestine. Chagall soon recognized that engravings were unworthy of the idea he now had of the formidable messianic epic, whose supernatural dimensions demanded a space (material and spiritual) wider than the copper plate, and a talent greater than that of the engraver. The impact of this epic did not immediately produce results. Almost twenty years later, during his second visit to Palestine, in 1951, the great inspiration flowered. The result was the tumultuous chromatism of the great historical canvases depicting the adventures of the Hebrew people: *Creation of Man* (1956–58); *King David* (1951); the episodes in the life of Moses, *Moses Receiving the Tablets of Law* (1950–52), *Moses Breaking the Tablets* (1955–56), and *Moses Leading the Twelve Tribes across the*

FLAYED OX. 1947
PRIVATE COLLECTION, PARIS

Gap in the Red Sea (1954–55). It is interesting to note that these paintings remain in the artist's possession. This would seem to indicate that the compositions have for him a meaning different from that which he attaches to his other pictures ; even if they do not count more, they are at least different—which underlines their exceptional place in the artist's work.

The different character of these works has not eliminated the usual figures who make up Chagall's plastic vocabulary. It is moving to meet again the personalities familiar since the Vitebsk period, and who are now associated with sacred episodes. It would have been incomprehensible had they been excluded. Their constant presence indicates how inseparable they are from the painter, and shows to what extent, both as ideas and as forms, they are part of his being. The scrannel-grating of the old street violinist takes up the refrain of the noble lyre of King David, regally attired in his red robe, while, clasping one another, the two immortal lovers of the Song of Songs cross the heavens leaving behind them the long trail of the Milky Way. In a corner of the picture the companions of his life—the painter with his palette and easel, the bearded pedlar carrying his bundle, the pied horse, the red cock in his golden halo—are gathered together to listen to the prophet.

All the themes are again collected in *The Creation of Man*. The most fantastic and incongruous are found beside those which call up some rational and logical association : the flying fish, the Vitebsk man walking with bowed head, Christ on the cross, the cock and the cow, a rabbi holding up at arm's length a seven-branched candelabra ; there is even the redoubtable devilish being wrapped in a blood-red robe, the satanic hybrid of ox and he-goat, that triumphed in 1911 in the picture paradoxically entitled *Dedicated to My Fiancée*. It would seem that

67

THE BIG CIRCUS. 1956

PRIVATE COLLECTION

the same piety which impels a primitive painter to add his own and his children's portrait to the foot of a sacred picture has encouraged Chagall to include in his epic Biblical histories the onlookers who have constantly accompanied him. But for all that, the atmosphere of miracle is not lessened or made mundane. The naively naturalist detail reintegrating the miracle into the daily world is not most important in the three great compositions of which Moses is the principal figure: most important is the originality of the composition and the prodigious evocation of the supernatural.

The spiritual tension is underlined by the force with which the various structural elements converge in an ascending movement, and by the simultaneous inspiration of the human complex by a divine breath, the pneuma, across a void filled with air which enables the planes of spirit and matter to communicate. It is the means generally employed by El Greco, with whom Chagall shows a singular relationship, principally noticeable in *The Burial of Count Orgaz* and in the different versions of *The Baptism of Christ,* particularly those of the Prado and the Hospital of San Juan Battista at Toledo. It is the ineffectual solution of the plastic problem of the interrelation of two universes of different nature, that leaves so many sacred paintings prosaic and sensual. In his Biblical epics Chagall has resolved this problem with a remarkable power of expression, which restores the actual character of the miraculous event with all its force and authority. The colossal figure of Moses, in the painting where he is breaking the tablets of the Law, almost fills the picture, towering towards the heaven which he seems to clasp with two arms, the better to bear witness and bring down the blessing of God on unworthy man.

In this composition Chagall appears as the most inspired and

70

THE COCK. 1947
PRIVATE COLLECTION. ▷

the most spiritual of all the painters who have essayed this formidable subject, not excluding Rembrandt and Tintoretto, nor Blake, whose technique often paralysed his monumental vision just when it was expressed in formal execution.

The same principle of vertical composition in *The Crossing of the Red Sea* arranges the rising mass of the Jewish people vertically, like a column with an angel as its capital, swirling upwards drawn by the Spirit of Redemption, signified on the one side by the Crucifixion, on the other by the temple of Jerusalem, while in the void the armies of Pharaoh collapse in death and founder as the waters swallow them up and engulf them in a vortex of downward movement contrasted with the ascending Hebrews. In Chagall's great religious paintings spirit becomes movement, and movement becomes spirit. Thus the work of Redemption is fulfilled, and sin is cleansed away through the labours of the Prophets waiting for the Messiah for whom Israel still hopes, and whom the Christians received in the person of Jesus.

Should Chagall's pictures in which the emblems and persons of the two religions are associated be interpreted in terms of a Judaio-Christian synthesis? If, for example, one enquires into *The White Crucifixion* (1938), *The Yellow Crucifixion* (1945), *The Blue Christ* (1950), or *The Descent from the Cross* (1950), one finds that in these pictures, which chronologically precede the Biblical epics, the figure of the crucified dominates. It is debatable whether the crucified is Jesus, the man who is God, the God-made man, or simply common man who personifies the suffering of the whole human race; or still more particularly, the Jew, pursued, hunted and martyred over thousands of years. In the last case the suffering of the Jewish people becomes the symbol of the suffering of the whole of humanity.

This meaning is clearly explicit in *The Martyr* (1940), where the crucified, who is no longer Jesus, but the Jew, wears on his head the everyday cap of the Jewish communities of Eastern Europe, the same cap as that worn by the bearded man who is reading at the foot of the Cross. This interpretation is confirmed and underlined by the fact that the martyr is wrapped in a veil which closely resembles a prayer shawl, a *thalith,* and all round him, as far as the horizon, the wooden houses of a little Russian Jewish village blaze, set alight during a pogrom.

The burning houses, the frenzied sectary who hurls his torch into the synagogue, the men shooting each other, the sinking boats, the trampled women, the escaping faithful who bear away the rolls of the Torah to save them from sacrilege— such are the themes inspired by the war and contemporary persecutions. They are found in paintings such as *The Resistance* (1937–48), *The Obsession* (1943), *The Spirit of the Town* (1945), and *The Fall of the Angel* (1922–33–47). Here Chagall interprets the miseries of the age, felt poignantly in flesh and spirit by all men who have experienced sorrow in the presence of modern barbarism. In these compositions people and things acquire a meaning which is more immediately obvious, more easily and clearly interpreted than the Chagall mythology of preceding years. On these scenes of suffering and death, the painter has lavished the furious chromatism of a palette where each colour glares with fiery intensity, shocks, burns, and echoes like a cry of indignation and suffering. The livid body bound to the cross, the crimson fire-cock who now fulfils his traditional function of arsonist, the poisonous yellows, acid blues, the gloom of night and the dark shadows of filth give these paintings a dramatic force even more gripping than the broad symphony of expanded magnificence of the Bible epics.

The pathetic, tragic prophecy which is one of the essential characteristics of the Bible evokes intense emotion in Chagall's work, whether the works illustrate the Holy Books directly, or

VILLAGE UNDER THE MOON. 1956
ROSENSAFT COLLECTION, MONTREUX

◁ BOUQUET WITH A GLASS OF WINE. 1953–54
ROSENSAFT COLLECTION, MONTREUX

whether they rediscover the constant tie with the life of the Jewish people through events of the contemporary scene. *The Obsession* (1943) is a canvas particularly representative of this indignant compassion. It collates the symbols of incurable human suffering, the burning *isbah,* the waggon harnessed for the flight of the frantic family, the candelabra with the broken candles, the inverted cross on the ground, the rioting mob and the collapsing church. The whole series of paintings inspired by the war, revolution, and persecution clearly links Chagall to the prophecy of wrath. He identifies himself with the man, Jeremiah perhaps, who is crouched on the soil, praying, meditating or reading, wrapped in his coat, the incarnation of solitude, distress, and desolation, who already in 1933 exhibits such moving grandeur in the picture entitled *Solitude.* The cosmopolitan Chagall, the "world citizen" who is equally at home in New York, Paris, or Vitebsk, has sent strong new roots deep into the fertile soil of the chosen people. Of his two souls, Russian and Jewish, it is the Jewish which waxes stronger, becomes more enlightened, and grows closer to truth.

There is yet another aspect of the Bible, very different from the prophecies of wrath and indignation, which moved the painter. He is responsible for so many "couples" and "lovers" inspired by the Song of Songs. Of all the books of Holy Scripture it is the most worldly and the closest to our passions, for it relates sensual love in burning verse. At the same time, following the oriental tradition found also in the Moslem mystics, it expresses the spirit dematerialized and divine love in terms analogous to those which sing of the union of flesh and desire triumphant.

In a splendid colour scheme whose sumptuous refined reds orchestrate its deep-toned warmth without any reference to local colour, the painter hurls the victorious cavalcade of entwined lovers into the air, whence they are carried off by the Pegasus of fairy tales and mythology *(Song of Songs,* version II, 1958). Or he may show a solitary lover reclining in an immense bouquet, floating above the sleeping town, a great naked planet around which mysterious constellations revolve.

This lyrical exaltation of passion, of desire, of tenderness, this eroticism at once ardent and pure, is also part of Chagall's own repertoire. It is only necessary to recall all his magnificent nudes, commencing with *The Red Nude* (1908), to understand the extent to which his sensibility and sensuality have always been animated by the spirit of the Song of Songs. The spirit moved him before he was ever inspired by the letter with which he does not, in any case, closely concern himself. From the appropriate treatment of each period, a special study of Chagall's nudes would lead to the discovery of the aesthetic and technical preoccupations which dominated him at that time. At one moment it might be graphic outline, structure and grouping of masses, at another fluid, sparkling chromatism, expressed in an explosion of overpowering passion, a firework lighting up the sky with bodies hurled into the Paris night like a flaming rocket of flesh (for example *The Red Nude* [1955]). Recall the gilded couple stretched on a cloud, huge, in a green-blue sky, gliding above a pale moon (1945); *The Snow* (1951), with its *isbahs* crushed by winter, its mythical animals watching over the slumber of the great snowy form, the snow fairy who fills the space with her nudity; *The Almond Trees* (1956), where the loving couple radiate an exquisite blue which makes the sparkling rose of the long flower branches stand out; remember all those lovers who from 1953 to 1955 wander embracing through Paris, and pass like meteors over the Seine

quays, over Notre-Dame, the Panthéon, and the Bastille column. Paris herself is, in Chagall's mind, a huge woman displayed in the phosphorescent night, a new wife full of surprises, flesh and spirit at the same time, over whom fly the childhood phantoms from Russia, whom the artist has brought with him and acclimatized to his adopted country.

THE REMBRANDT CONTEXT

The curious phrase " *Je suis certain que Rembrandt m'aime* " from Chagall's autobiography, following that in which he declares himself a stranger to Soviet Russia as much as to that of the Czars, takes on a strong, very moving meaning. One would not think from first contact with this painter's work that his "spiritual home", the source of his replenishment and his constant study, would be the work of Rembrandt. But on reflection, no artist is as close to Chagall as the Dutchman who described his inner world with such feverish poetry, through the means of beings and objects which surrounded him. In Rembrandt, as with Chagall, the objectivity that one admires is nothing other than an effusion of spirit that saturates and infuses into matter a mysterious light which shines through the most opaque surfaces. It is an objectivity which is concerned only with the object, whether it be a gift of experience or an invention of imagination.

It is possible that Chagall recalled the skinned ox of the Louvre when he painted his carcasses of 1929 and 1947 ; the first is hung before a quiet countryside while the second, at which the ritual butcher charges in full flight, knife in hand, presents the solemn drama of a sacrifice. Here also the *clarté*

79

THE RED NUDE. 1954–55
ROSENSAFT COLLECTION, MONTREUX

of which Maritain speaks is, as with Rembrandt, an internal clarity, the perfect equilibrium of fantasy and reason, of dreams and reality. It is a power that dominates the crowd of phantoms who slide into all his pictures and stir up the canvas with their strange rustlings. Neither summoned nor rejected, they are there as products of memory—remembered portraits. Nothing is more explicit in this respect than *Appearance of the Artist's Family* (1935–47), which remains in the painter's private collection, together with all the pictures that mean most to him, whether as spiritual adventures, or as exceptionally rewarding examples of his art and work.

The dream atmosphere lends this composition an enigmatic brilliance which is reinforced by the wonderful depth and truly visionary incandescence of the blues and reds. Most of the familiar characters are there: the man who clasps the Torah to his breast; Chagall's mother; the little boy who skips over the roofs of Vitebsk as though on a springboard; his fiancée flourishing her bouquet; the angel falling from the sky with his book open, the angel of the apocalypse, his guardian angel, the inspirer of the evangelist; the crowd of brothers and sisters jostling one another in the old family hall; the amicable cow. All this is set in the middle of the sky above the sleeping town, one half of which reflects the red light of a conflagration while the other half glows with an idyllic blue. As in so many other pictures which show him in front of his easel—*Self-Portrait with a Clock, The Spirit of the Town* (1945), *Between Dog and Wolf* (1938–42), and *The Black Glove* (1923–48)— the painter represents the real or unreal characters which pass at that moment before his mind's eye and confer that special poetry of his on the picture.

The spectator is inclined to regard them as enigmas, as

81

THE BIG NUDE WITH THE BASKET. 1955
◁ HANS SCHRODER COLLECTION, SARREBRUCK

bizarre characters whose effective presence or haunting memory may be rediscovered in Courbet's *Studio* (of which the *Appearance of the Artist's Family* appears as a paraphrase), but for the painter himself there is nothing enigmatic about them. This is so because for him material and supernatural reality are indistinguishable, to such an extent do they possess the same density and an equally real existence. No more than Rembrandt, "whom he knows loves him", has Chagall put a frontier between the rational and the miraculous. On the contrary, he has so well mixed their substance, that they both appear as witnesses to the same truth. One does not desire to contest the authenticity of Chagall's visions any more than those of William Blake, since they are only another means through which reality reveals itself to the painter's view.

It is this simplicity, this kind of infantile innocence, in which he bathes in the *saine clarté* of his visionary approach, that makes Chagall unique in the art of his time. He is as far from the Realists as from the Surrealists; he is the sole master of his magic laboratory, where it is brilliant, fluid colour that comes before the demands of the imagination and leads in the flights of fancy. The total extent of his activity, which has already spanned half a century, is unique. During this period, through his incredible capacity for self-refreshment and his inexhaustible fecundity, possessed by few contemporary painters, he has constantly developed and changed. His different stages of development follow each other with a truly natural rhythm, with apparently no misgivings about problems of form and its representation. They are like the flowering of a garden, like the songs of a bird. Yet look at them carefully; what a wily old bird, what a vigorous, carefully cultivated garden.

LIST OF ILLUSTRATIONS